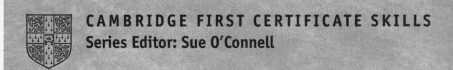

CAMBRIDGE FIRST CERTIFICATE SKILLS

Series Editor: Sue O'Connell

CAMBRIDGE FIRST CERTIFICATE

Reading

NEW EDITION

Paul Roberts

Teacher's Book

CAMBRIDGE
UNIVERSITY PRESS

PUBLISHED BY THE PRESS SYNDICATE OF THE UNIVERSITY OF CAMBRIDGE
The Pitt Building, Trumpington Street, Cambridge, United Kingdom

CAMBRIDGE UNIVERSITY PRESS
The Edinburgh Building, Cambridge CB2 2RU, UK
40 West 20th Street, New York, NY 10011–4211, USA
10 Stamford Road, Oakleigh, VIC 3166, Australia
Ruiz de Alarcón 13, 28014 Madrid, Spain
Dock House, The Waterfront, Cape Town 8001, South Africa

http://www.cambridge.org

© Cambridge University Press 1994, 1999

First published 1994
Second edition 1999
Reprinted 2001

Printed in the United Kingdom at the University Press, Cambridge

ISBN 0 521 64655 3 Teacher's Book
ISBN 0 521 64656 1 Student's Book

Contents

Introduction 1

Foundation unit 3

1 The fun they had 8

2 Choosing a college place 11

3 Schools keep boys and girls apart 14

4 Defending your territory on the beach 17

5 How green was my holiday? 20

6 A holiday in the Caribbean 23

7 The lion cub 27

8 Zooooooh! 30

9 A different point of view 33

10 How to get a laugh 36

11 Superstar 39

12 Success in a man's world 43

13 Film reviews 46

14 Goodbye to film heroes 49

15 How to be a movie star 53

Review unit 56

Practice tests 59

Practice test 1 60

Practice test 2 63

Practice test 3 66

Practice test 4 69

Practice test 5 72

Introduction

Who is this book for?

Cambridge First Certificate Reading is for learners who need additional practice in reading skills in preparation for Paper 1 of the Cambridge First Certificate in English (FCE) examination. As the book aims to improve learners' reading skills in general, as well as specifically for the exam, it can also be used appropriately by non-exam learners at upper intermediate level who want to develop their reading ability.

How is it organised?

The *Student's Book* is organised into learning units and practice tests. The learning units present different techniques for acquiring useful reading skills and the practice tests provide an opportunity to test those skills in the context of Paper 1 of the FCE exam.

There are fifteen learning units and five practice tests. In addition, a Foundation unit at the beginning presents the subskills necessary for developing and improving reading skills at this level and a Review unit at the end summarises and consolidates all the reading techniques presented in the book. Five broad themes run through all the learning units and practice tests, loosely linking the material together.

Each learning unit focuses on a different set of reading skills and on a specific part of the Paper 1 exam. Summary boxes at the beginning of each unit give clear information about the unit's skills and exam coverage and provide cross-references to relevant practice test material. Exam tip boxes in every unit provide a useful summary of key techniques.

The practice test material closely resembles Paper 1 of the FCE exam and includes examples of all variations of the exam format.

The *Teacher's Book* contains a timing guide for each unit, detailed teaching notes and a key to the unit exercises and practice tests.

How should the material be used?

The learning units are intended to be used in sequence because reading techniques and exam skills are built up gradually and an element of recycling and revision is incorporated into the book. It is, however, possible to choose individual units for particular skills practice or particular exam part practice, as each unit is self-contained and can stand alone. Each learning unit provides between 40 and 60 minutes' work.

Introduction

The practice tests can be used flexibly, in conjunction with or independently of the learning units. Test parts can be used in any order, individually or as a complete test:

- to check progress or to provide authentic timed exam practice.
- after every four learning units or at other intervals throughout the course.
- for homework or in class.
- with students working individually or in pairs/groups.

Note for teachers

The choice of texts in the book aims to reflect the variety and balance of text types used in the FCE examination. The texts are all taken from authentic sources and have been edited for length, but are otherwise unchanged except:

1 Occasional words have been replaced with synonyms. This has been done so as to bring the vocabulary within Level 5 of Hindmarsh's *Cambridge English Lexicon* – used as a general guide for FCE materials and Parts 1–3 of the examination itself.

2 The texts in Part 2 of Practice Tests 4 and 5 have been taken from books intended for a British youth readership. One or two adjustments have been made to these texts where, in the original, the language was too culturally specific for most EFL students.

The methodology of the reading activities is intended to be communicative and process-oriented. Where, in the exam, a reason for reading is given (Part 4), this is taken into consideration in the methodology. Otherwise there is no emphasis on reasons for reading, nor is there any attempt to introduce text topics in advance of the texts themselves, reflecting the reality of reading under examination conditions.

Foundation unit

The overall aim of this unit is to introduce the text and exercise types in the book and to emphasise the *process* orientation of the material. The boxed sections with the heading 'First Certificate Exam' in this unit link activities to the FCE exam. Most of the boxed tips in the other units of the book can be related back to these boxed sections. Allow about 90 minutes for this unit.

What sort of things do you read?

There are two aims to this activity. The first is to make students aware, or to heighten their awareness, of different text types and of the fact that we read them for different purposes. (Text types are sometimes referred to as 'genres'.) The second aim is to introduce all the reading material in the book and to make it 'user-friendly' by encouraging familiarity with it from the beginning of the course.

Start by showing students real examples of some of the text types. Bring, for example, a real newspaper, a novel, a brochure and a non-fiction book to the lesson. It doesn't matter if these are not in English.

Allow students ten minutes to go through the book. Encourage students to discuss why they think each text belongs to a particular type. Remind them to think about the layout, presentation and typeface of each text and the use of pictures.

KEY

Text type	Page number
newspaper article	55, 62
non-fiction book	19, 43, 67
magazine article	23, 27, 40, 48, 60
story	11, 35
brochure	15, 32
biography	51

Allow five minutes for the discussion of the four questions. Encourage students to talk about what they read in their own language, as well as in English.

If you have a set of class readers or your students use a library, this would be a good moment to have them choose something to read. Ask students to explain their choice.

Different kinds of reading

The aim of this section is to introduce students to the two widely diverging styles of reading required by the FCE examination. In Parts 1–3 of the examination, the requirement is to read for understanding, whereas in Part 4 candidates have to read in order to obtain information.

Allow students five minutes to have the preliminary discussion which should lead to an awareness of the two styles of reading.

You may need to spend a little time explaining more thoroughly the difference between the two styles but students should begin to grasp the difference by filling in the chart.

KEY	
Things we read like a novel	*Things we read like a timetable*
novel	timetable
magazine article	encyclopaedia entry
research article	guide book
newspaper article	manual
letter from a friend	brochure
biography	

Obviously there could be some useful debate about the items in the chart: it is possible, for example, to read a newspaper article for information, especially if you just want some facts and figures; it is doubtful, however, that anyone would read a timetable for the pleasure of doing so or to find out the writer's point of view.

How can you become a better reader?

The aim of this section is to introduce the six strategies which will enable students to become better readers. These strategies are all developed in the rest of the book. They are:

1 Dealing with difficult words
2 Ignoring irrelevant information
3 Getting an overall picture
4 Responding to the text
5 Analysing the text
6 Keeping your purpose in mind

1 Dealing with difficult words

Ask students to work in pairs and to discuss the probable meanings of the invented words. Allow ten minutes for pairwork and then discuss the meanings of the words with the class.

KEY

1 *blistable* stands before *radio*, so it must be an adjective. It ends in *-able*, so this means that you can *blist* the radio. What can you do with certain types of radio? You can carry them, fold them, convert them into other things. It could mean *portable, collapsible* or *convertible*, for example.
2 *squarked* ends in *-ed* so is probably a verb. After arriving in a taxi, you get out. So *squarked* probably means the same as *got out*.
3 *flort* is more difficult. The reference to the door shows that Stella knew where she was going, so *flort* cannot be a place, because, if it were, it would be *the flort*. So it is probably a time expression, meaning a short space of time, e.g. *moment* or *flash*.
4 *plinge* must refer to something you can do with your hair. She seems to be going somewhere important so *plinge* probably means *comb* or *brush*.

---

2 Ignoring irrelevant information

Keep students in pairs to work on the advertisement. Limit their time strictly. Two or three minutes should be easily enough: the point of the exercise is to show that, when you are reading for information, you can ignore unknown words which are not connected with your purpose. Students are not expected to know all of the words in the exercise, but they can still answer the question.

KEY

It costs nothing to change oil.

---

3 Getting an overall picture

After one or two minutes stop students from trying to answer the questions. (The point is that it is impossible to answer the questions before looking at the picture.) Then tell students to look at the picture on page 6.

Allow a further few minutes to find the correct answers.

KEY

1 The *correct floor* is the third/top floor.
2 The *whole operation* is the 'serenading' of the young woman.
3 *that far* is from the ground to the top floor.

---

4 Responding to the text

Ask students to work through the activity individually. You could run this activity as a competition to see who reaches the right answer (Mexico City) first.

Allow about ten minutes for the discussion on responses to different text types. The discussion should be as 'open' as possible – allow students to match as many text types to each response as they want to, as long as they can justify their choice. Encourage them to talk about things they have read to illustrate their point of view.

5 Analysing the text

Allow ten minutes for this task. Ask students to do the activity individually and then discuss their answers when they have made their decisions.

KEY

1 d) Because
2 a) Therefore
3 *the event* is the restaurant meal the people want to complain about.

---

6 Keeping your purpose in mind

Allow students a few minutes to read the text and to answer the question. Do not allow students to spend too long on the text: the point is for them to find out that, if they had been given the purpose first, they could have gone through the text much faster.

KEY

The Park Ranger work lasts five months.

Testing your progress – The First Certificate in English exam

Paper 1 in the exam

The aim of this section is to give students basic information about Paper 1 in the exam. Allow five minutes for them to read through and then take some time to focus on the timing implications: if 75 minutes are allowed for the examination, students should allow fifteen minutes for each part and a further fifteen minutes for checking.

Practice tests

The aim of this activity is to help students to see how the FCE works in practice and to familiarise them with the format of the practice tests so that they will be prepared for them.

Allow ten minutes for this activity.

KEY

1 There are 35 questions in total.
2 Parts 1, 3 and 4 have an example – 0.
3 Parts 1 and 3 have an extra answer which you do not need to use.
4 In Part 4, you can use an answer more than once.
5 Part 4 sometimes has more than one answer for the same question (e.g. Practice Test 2, 23 and 24, 34 and 35, on page 92).

Optional extension

Ask students to read the 'First Certificate Exam' boxes in this unit again, and suggest they start a 'reading record' based on them. Tell students to record, as they read their readers or other materials, how they deal with new words, how they form an overall picture, how they respond to each text, how they keep their purpose in mind and ignore irrelevant information, and if they have to analyse any part of the text.

Unit 1 **The fun they had**

Discuss with students the aims of Unit 1 – these are stated in the box at the beginning of each learning unit. Remind students of the relevant sections in the Foundation unit.

Getting an overall picture

It is important to get students into the habit of looking quickly at or through a text in order to get a picture of it or a framework within which to understand it properly.

1 Give your students one minute only to do the first activity; make sure you time them rigorously. You could make the activity into a competition – the first person to spot the recurrent words is the winner.

KEY

The recurrent words students should find are *school* and *teacher*.

---

2 Allow students five minutes to address the discussion question and to complete the chart. It does not matter if what students write in their charts has nothing to do with what the story is about – the important thing is that they have a good opportunity to think about the theme. In a class discussion, find out if students think schools will be better or worse in 2157 or about the same.

Dealing with difficult words

All the activities on page 12 require students to read the text in short sections and to stop and think after each section. Emphasise to students that it is always important to pause for thought while reading. You could explain that it is like an underwater swimmer coming up for air.

1 Allow students five minutes to read and discuss the four questions.

KEY

1 Margie and Tommy
2 some sort of electronic book or talking book, perhaps
3 very old
4 She was excited enough to write it in her diary – with an exclamation mark.

---

2 Allow a further ten minutes for the reading, underlining and discussion. Students may be puzzled at having to underline everything they understand, especially as underlining unknown words is such a common practice. Reassure them by pointing out that they will still be able to see, quite clearly, the words they have not understood.

Students may do this underlining in different ways: some will underline word for word, some will underline continuously as they read, some will read, stop and underline. If there are all three varieties of student in the class, point out that the third system (reading, stopping and underlining) is the most efficient.

When they come to comparing texts with their partners, give students time to discuss and share knowledge about words.

The purpose of the whole operation is to give them confidence by showing them how much they understand rather than undermine their confidence by pointing up what they do not understand.

Responding to the text

1 Allow five minutes for students to pick out the dialogue between Margie and Tommy.

KEY

She said, 'Where did you find it?'

'In my house.' He pointed without looking, because he was busy reading. 'In the cellar.'

'What's it about?'

'School.'

Margie was scornful. 'School? What's there to write about school? I hate school … Why would anyone write about school?'

Tommy looked at her with very superior eyes. 'Because it's not our kind of school, stupid. This is the old kind of school that they had hundreds and hundreds of years ago.' He added grandly, pronouncing the word carefully, 'Centuries ago.'

Margie was hurt. 'Well, I don't know what kind of school they had all that time ago.' She read the book over his shoulder for a while, then said, 'Anyway, they had a teacher.'

---

2 Allow five minutes for students to read the dialogue aloud. If there are any students in the class who particularly enjoy play-acting, ask them to perform for the whole class while the others decide which tones are most appropriate.

Direct students towards the words they have circled in order to decide on appropriate tones.

Although the activity should be seen as fun, it is important to make the serious point that efficient reading requires the reader to read between the lines and to get at thoughts and feelings which are not necessarily explicitly stated.

Exam practice: Part 2 Multiple choice comprehension questions

This activity is simply to start students off in getting used to Part 2 style questions.

Allow ten minutes for students to finish reading the text and to answer the question. Make sure students try to answer the question before looking at the four given answers. You could tell them to close their books while you dictate the question to avoid their looking at the answers.

KEY

The correct answer is C. There is no indication that Margie doesn't like arithmetic (A). The reference to Margie's sigh is immediately followed by a reference to her thinking about schools – if her sigh was because of frustration at not being able to read more (B) or because of the argument with Tommy (D), it would have occurred earlier, or the final paragraph would have referred to this.

Extension

Apart from reflecting on the text, students can use this discussion to talk about how they approach studying for their English examinations.

If there is time after pairwork discussion, you could ask students to report back to the whole class.

Unit 2 Choosing a college place

Begin by asking students how they are getting on with their general reading and if they are using the exam tips given in Unit 1. Remind them of these tips, if necessary.

Discuss the aims of Unit 2 with students. Reassure them that *one- or two-word summaries* will soon become clear and point out that highlighting and underlining are straightforward and self-explanatory.

Make sure students know what a college brochure is. If possible bring a brochure in to show them. It doesn't have to be in English.

Keeping your purpose in mind

1 Allow students ten minutes to think about the question and then to discuss their answers in pairs.

2 Keep students in pairs to do the matching activity. You may want to explain *Catering* (providing food for large numbers of people) or you may want students to use a dictionary to find out its meaning.

Allow five minutes for the activity.

KEY

1 Children
2 Entrance qualifications
3 Catering
4 Work experience
5 Management

---

3 The aim of the reading race is to help students to get into the habit of 'scan-reading' – running their eyes as quickly as possible over the text in order to find specific information. It should not take more than one minute.

KEY

The first section of the brochure is all about *access courses* which lead to *the qualifications they need in order to enter higher education.*

Ignoring irrelevant information

Remind students that they should now read the whole text in the same way as they read for the race – as quickly as possible, looking out only for words and phrases connected to the summarised purposes. Allow five to ten minutes for the activity.

KEY

Underlined or highlighted sections:

All Bedford College access courses are recognised nationally as giving successful students the qualifications they need in order to enter higher education …

These include courses in general management, accountancy, personnel, marketing, purchasing and supply, quality management, administrative management …

Our expanding range of catering courses offers you the opportunity either to take a broad path developing practical and supervisory skills …

Caring for children in the home, in hospital and in residential settings, nurseries and schools requires trained people. With our range of courses you have the best of all possible worlds …

During your course you will have the opportunity to visit particular companies to enable you to relate your studies to current industrial practices …

Exam practice: Part 4 Multiple matching

This activity introduces a Part 4 style task and consolidates the previous task. You may need to remind students that in the exam they will have only to write numbers against purposes, rather than write out the headings of the relevant sections of text.

KEY

1 Health and leisure
2 Access courses
3 Creative arts
4 Technology
5 Advanced and professional

Extension

The purpose of the Extension is, as always, to provide students with some speaking practice as a change from the reading and study focus of the rest of the unit and to round off the topic.

You could organise the first discussion 'pyramid style': allow students five minutes or so to work in pairs and to put the criteria in order. Then, combine pairs to make groups of four students who have to agree on the order of the criteria. After a few minutes, combine fours to make groups of eight.

Unit 3 Schools keep boys and girls apart

Begin by asking students what they can remember of the exam tips so far. You could set up a quick pairwork discussion, where students swap experiences from their general reading. Remind them again of the importance of keeping a 'reading record'.

Look at the aims of the unit with students. Reference words are usually grammatical words such as *it*, *there* and *do/does/did* which refer back to previously mentioned things.

Getting an overall picture

Allow five minutes for the discussion, but make sure students do *not* refer to the text for their answers.

The illustration and layout should indicate the text type (non-fiction book) to students. As usual, it is not important if, in answering question 2, the students do not mention anything dealt with in the text.

Responding to the text

You may need to remind students of the 'underlining-what-you-understand' technique and of the importance of pausing to 'come up for air' while reading.

Allow ten minutes for the reading and discussion. There are, of course, no right answers.

Analysing the text

1 Remind students that text analysis is often necessary in order to tackle the gapped text task in Part 3. It is also sometimes necessary for answering the multiple choice comprehension questions in Part 2.

2 Allow five to ten minutes for the discussion.

KEY

1 *nor* shows an alternative, a second of two possibilities in a negative statement; *or* does the same thing but in a positive statement – *either (...) or (...)* and *neither (...) nor (...)*
2 *it* refers to *Such male-oriented teaching*
3 *do* can be replaced by *take many mathematics and science courses*

---

3 This activity requires students to circle reference words and then to draw lines to indicate what they refer to. Students could do the activity individually or in pairs, with discussion. Allow about ten minutes.

KEY

The marked-up text should look like this:

If there is no difference in general intelligence between boys and girls, what can explain girls' lack of success in [science and mathematics] ?

It seems to be that their treatment at school is a direct cause. Mathematics and science are seen as mainly masculine subjects, and therefore, as [girls] become teenagers, they are less likely to take them.

However, if we examine the performance of boys and girls who have undertaken mathematics courses, there are still more high-achieving boys than there are girls. [This difference] appears to be world-wide (see graph). Biological explanations have been offered for this, but there are other explanations too.

[Evidence shows that exceptional mathematicians and scientists have not had teachers who supplied answers]

Apart from that, there can be little doubt that teachers of [mathematics and science] expect their male students to do better at these subjects than their female students. *3 They even appear to encourage the difference between the sexes. They spend more time with the [male students], giving them longer to answer questions and working harder to get correct responses from them. They are more likely to call on boys for answers and to allow them to take the lead in classroom discussion. They also praise boys more frequently. All of this tends to encourage boys to work harder in science and mathematics and to give them confidence that they are able to succeed. *4

Such male-oriented teaching is not likely to encourage girls to take many mathematics and science courses, nor is it likely to support girls who do.

Exam practice: Part 3 Gapped text

This activity introduces a Part 3 style task and leads on from the text analysis section: tell students to use the same analysis techniques to look at reference words in the four sentences and to relate them to relevant items in the text, at the numbered points.

Allow five to ten minutes for the activity.

KEY

1 D
2 A
3 B
4 C

Extension

Allow five minutes for this discussion. Encourage students to use some of the language from the text.

Unit 4 Defending your territory on the beach

Discuss the aims of Unit 4 with students. Explain that 'having a conversation' with the writer is another form of responding to the text – it involves students reading short sections of the text at a time, summarising them and then asking (mainly rhetorical) questions to check understanding. The 'conversation' takes place as students consult the section of text to confirm the substance of their questions.

Getting an overall picture

1 Allow five minutes for pairwork discussion of the four questions. Then discuss them together.

The wording of the title (*Defending your territory*) suggests a military context. Discussion of questions 1 and 2 should, therefore, revolve around the area of war. People normally defend territory by fighting.

When students are discussing the third question, try to introduce some of the vocabulary of the text – words like *boundaries, territorial marker* and *territorial marking powers*.

2 These discussion points are simply aimed at getting students to think about the theme of the text. It is important at this stage, as with similar activities in other units, not to lead students to the ideas in the text, but just to let them discuss their own ideas.

Dealing with difficult words

Remind students that they can often achieve a good understanding of a text by simply avoiding difficult words (as they did in Unit 1 on page 12).

Allow a few minutes for them to read the section on *passers-by* and make sure they understand the explanation. Tell students to find the five words or expressions from the list in the text and work out the meaning, if necessary, by dividing them into different parts. If students need help while they are reading, you could help them individually as follows:

belongings (line 2) You know the verb *belong*. If things belong to you, they are your *belongings*.

air-beds (line 3) What is *air*? What are *beds*? *Air-beds* are beds (mattresses) with air in them.

equidistant (line 23) You know what *distant* means. What do the letters *equ* suggest? Can you think of some words (*equal/equality/equation*) beginning with *equ*? So *equidistant* means at an equal distance.

by-passed (lines 49–50) You know what *passers-by* means. A passer-by *by-passes* things!

thereafter (line 55) You know the meaning of *there* and *after*. So *thereafter* means after that moment.

Responding to the text

Allow fifteen minutes for these activities. Their aim is to give students practice in summarising as they read. This skill is particularly important for students to develop in order to complete the multiple matching task in Part 1 of the exam.

1 Give students enough time to read the first paragraph carefully. You could choose two students to read the dialogue aloud to the rest of the class. Make sure the class sees that the tone of the text is mildly critical, although it is written in a scientific, 'objective' way.

2 After students have read the second paragraph, you will probably need to have some 'cross-class' conversations, until students get the idea of role-playing conversations. Then let students work in closed pairs.

KEY

A possible continuation of the dialogue:

Reader: Well what did you mean?

Writer: Almost the opposite: most families are over-prepared for a day on the beach.

---

3 In order to set students off reading and role-playing the other paragraphs, you could revise 'acknowledging' and 'rejecting' language (for example, *Yes, you could say that's what I meant./No, that's not it at all.*).

KEY

A possible conversation for the third paragraph:

Reader: In your opinion people want to show they own their place on the beach.

Writer: Yes, you could say that's what I meant. But first they do make sure they *can* own it.

Reader: You mean by checking exactly where it should be?

Writer: Yes, that's what I meant by working out the appropriate spot.

Exam practice: Part 1 Multiple matching

This activity introduces a Part 1 style task. If students have completed the role-playing tasks on page 24 they should have a clear idea about the theme of each paragraph, so the matching task should be very straightforward. Allow students five minutes to complete it.

KEY

1 F The *range of personal belongings that individuals take with them* makes a trip to the beach a major expedition.

2 B Families take all their things to the beach *to mark out the new territorial boundaries of this family group*. In other words, it is a matter of personal space.

3 D The paragraph is about *calculations* (mathematics), *claiming the land, like Columbus* (conquest) and being *watched very carefully* (an alert eye).

4 A *I decided to try* indicates that this was an experiment.

5 C The convincing performance is the towel's success as *an extremely effective territorial marker*.

6 E The paragraph is all about how the towel lost its power.

Extension

The aim of the extension is to give some extra speaking practice, using the vocabulary in the text.

Allow five minutes for the discussion.

KEY

3 People often defend territory on trains by putting books or magazines on the seat, while in libraries and cinemas, many people put jackets or coats on seats.

Unit 5 How green was my holiday?

The aims in the box should all be fairly familiar. 'Reference words' were introduced in Unit 3: they are the words in a text which refer back to other words or ideas.

Getting an overall picture

1 The aim of the activity is to revise techniques for getting an overall picture.

Students should be getting used to looking at the text for one minute only by now, but you may still find you have to time them rigorously.

2 Allow between five and ten minutes for the discussion on the text. This should be quite open. Only the first question has an unequivocal answer which is that the picture is a representation of the USA in the form of a lake in the mountains – a national park. It is important that students get the chance to discuss which technique works best for this type of text, as well as the ideas in the text.

Analysing the text

Students will probably need about fifteen minutes to do these activities.

1 To make sure students see what the reference words refer to, you could write on the board:

1 That's certainly how they see themselves.
2 Practical down-to-earth no-nonsense types is certainly how Americans think of themselves.

You could then make the point that sentence 2 can be understood on its own while sentence 1 needs to follow a preceding sentence in order to make sense.

Give students some time to think about and connect up the reference words in the last sentence of paragraph 1 and check they have got the right idea. You could show them the correct solution on the board.

> **KEY**
>
> What [Americans] like most is [a good, wide-ranging philosophical argument, plus a crisis]. (They) have invented (both) for their national parks system.

2 Make sure that students have identified the correct sentences. Allow five minutes for the task.

KEY

1 [Too many people are visiting the system – up to almost 400 million last year. It's said they are ruining the plants with the pollution from their cars, scaring the animals, destroying by their numbers the wilderness experience the parks are suppose to offer.] ←
   It's hard for a visitor from Europe to feel (that way).
2 The busiest park in the system, the Great Smoky Mountains between Tennessee and North Carolina, can get [60,000 visitors on a single summer's day]. (That) sounds plenty and it is.
3 [There's a video rental store now and even a small prison, for visitors who get drunk and disorderly]. In spite of (this), the main environmental threat is smog drifting east from Los Angeles.
4 Should [the accommodation] be so basic that only true lovers of nature will be tempted to come? Or should (it) contain – as it increasingly does – en suite bathrooms and colour TVs?

Dealing with difficult words

Allow ten to fifteen minutes for these activities.

The aim is to show students a technique which can complement the technique of breaking words down into parts which was introduced in the previous unit.

KEY

1 People are apparently destroying the *wilderness experience*. They are destroying it simply by being present in large numbers. The *wilderness experience* therefore means the experience of being somewhere a long way from human population.
2 You might expect to see forests, animals, mountains, etc., in a national park. You would expect mountains to have snow on them and you would expect them to be in the background. The *range of the Tetons* is a group of mountains.
3 A *hands-off policy* means leaving things to nature and not interfering. Animals face the danger, in winter, of dying because they do not have enough food. So *starve* means 'die through lack of food'.

Exam practice: Part 2 Multiple choice comprehension questions

Allow students ten to fifteen minutes to read through the text and answer the questions.

KEY

1 B The text analysis work on the reference word *both* on page 26 should have led students to this answer. Americans are seen here as the opposite of *no-nonsense* (A). They have invented an argument *and* a crisis (C). *both* does not refer to parks (D).

2 D This sentence, taken with the question, is more or less a paraphrase of a sentence students should have arrived at during the text analysis activity on page 28. The writer emphasises that pollution and destruction levels are talked about – but hard to perceive (A, C). In paragraph 4 the writer describes how easy it was to get into the wilderness (B).

3 A *you are necessarily excluding America's growing population of old people* indicates that elderly people would not be able to stay in the parks. *the former* refers to basic accommodation.

4 D Students should have arrived at this answer during the text analysis activity on page 28.

Extension

Allow students five minutes for this discussion. The writer's point of view is slightly unusual in that he does not seem to be particularly alarmed or worried about environmental problems. You might like to set questions 3 and 4 as essay titles.

Unit 6 A holiday in the Caribbean

Discuss the aims with the students. Ask them what techniques they can remember. *Dealing with difficult words* revises and extends previous work in this area.

You could bring a real brochure to show the class (it doesn't have to be in English) and remind them of the different way you normally read a brochure, compared with, say, a newspaper article or a story.

Dealing with difficult words

1 Allow about ten minutes for this activity. Remind students of the technique of dividing words up. The example word used in Unit 4 (see page 23) was *passers-by*.

KEY

The word *overhang* can easily be divided into *over* and *hang*.

1 The beautiful beaches are *far away* – a long way away.
2 The twin volcanoes *mark* out the *land* – they are a feature which can be seen from many different places and which can help you to know where you are.
3 The *coastline* is the *line* which the *coast* follows.
4 *Woodland* is *land* covered in *woods* or forests.
5 The reefs are not on the shore – they are *off* the *shore*, or just a little way out into the sea.

2–3 Allow ten minutes for these activities.

The aim of these activities is to show students that they can often make a guess at the meaning of a word by thinking about its root. You might like to make the point that this is not always possible and that some words do not mean what their apparent root might make you think they mean. Make sure students understand that they should also use the context to work out a word's meaning.

2

KEY

1 b) *captive* is the root of the word – leading to the *held* meaning of *captivated*. The context shows that meaning b) is the only sensible one.
2 d) *grandeur* contains the root *grand* which has to do with size, rather than variety, riches or beauty.
3 a) *contentment* contains the word *content*, meaning 'happy'.

3

KEY

1 extremely well-known – people have talked about them so much and even written books about them that they have become a *legend*
2 robbery involving *pirates* – colourful men who used to attack ships and steal everything they were carrying
3 very well *lit* at night time – the courts are *flooded* in light

---

Keeping your purpose in mind and ignoring irrelevant information

Remind students that these techniques are relevant only to Part 4 of the examination, and for reading texts for information purposes only.

1 This activity builds on the activity in Unit 2 where students had to match given key words to different purposes. Here they have to find their own key words for each purpose. Allow five minutes for this.

KEY

Possible answers:
1 market
2 golf
3 beach
4 civilisation/nature

---

2 Allow a further two or three minutes for students to 'scan' and highlight or underline the text, and five minutes for comparing differences and answering the questions.

KEY

The underlined sections of text should be:

St. Lucia
St. Lucia is undeveloped (as are its roads and services!) and while it remains unspoilt

Antigua
Antigua has a beach for every day of the year
the market is a battlefield where gossip is exchanged with goods

Jamaica
Jamaica has it all. The sugar-white sands of the north coast resorts are legendary
play golf on a number of world class courses

Barbados
Barbados is blessed with beautiful beaches
with championship golf

1 B
2 C, D
3 B, C, D
4 A

Exam practice: Part 4 Multiple matching

This exam-style activity should now be very straightforward. Students will simply have to repeat the process in the previous task, coming up with one- or two-word summaries, underlining or highlighting sections of the text relevant to the questions and then filling in the boxes. Ten minutes should be enough time for the activity. You could reinforce the point that students did not have to read the brochure thoroughly in order to complete the task.

KEY

1 B	2 D	3 D	4 A	5 A
6 C	7 B	8 D	9 A	10 C

The underlined sections of the text should be:

St. Lucia
dramatic scenery
the friendliest people in the Caribbean
a spicy traditional cuisine

Antigua
the gentle pace, infectious calm and general contentment
wooden balconies a century old overhang the street

Jamaica
as scenic as any island you will find
a wide choice of water-based activity

Barbados
the characteristic music of steel bands, the cool sound of jazz and the
more relaxed Latin American rhythms
classical colonial plantation mansions
the time-honoured tradition of taking life slowly

Extension

This is an open-ended activity which could lead to a lot of discussion.
You could organise it 'pyramid fashion': allow students five minutes to
discuss in pairs; then put pairs together to form groups of four, allowing
a further five minutes to reach an agreement. Continue with larger
groups.

Unit 7 **The lion cub**

The items in the aims box should be clear.

Getting an overall picture

1 Allow five to ten minutes for this activity.

Encourage the students to summarise the beginning of the story before looking at the phrases.

<table>
<tr><td>

KEY

One day a man came into the surgery with a lion cub. He looked very proud. A few weeks later I went with Maurice to the zoo to see the same lion cub.

</td></tr>
</table>

2 Allow five minutes for the discussion. Remind students not to look for answers in the text. The discussion, as with all discussions at this stage in a unit, is to get ideas flowing. It does not matter if students' answers are right or wrong – they will have the opportunity to see how right they are later on. What is important is that students discuss the text so far and think of as many feasible possibilities as they can. However, Maurice cannot be a zoo-keeper since he would not have *a morning at the zoo*.

Responding to the text

Allow ten minutes for this activity. You may need to review the meanings of the adjectives before students attempt the activity. The adjective *sympathetic*, in particular, may be a problem as it is a 'false friend' in many languages.

Clearly there are no absolute right answers – the important thing is that students concentrate on the text and their reactions to it and support their reactions with quotations from the text.

KEY

Possible answers:

Maurice	*	*Supporting phrase*
worried	4	it would be very difficult ...
severe	2	They did, did they?
businesslike	8	I'll ask the manager of our local zoo if ...
sympathetic	7	I'm afraid so.

Man with cub		
proud	1	Only twelve weeks old and tough as they come
enthusiastic	3	We're great animal lovers ...
confused	5	But what on earth ...
shocked	6	The man stared down ...

Analysing the text

This section revises the technique of analysing texts by using reference words (introduced in Unit 3 and also featured in Unit 5) and presents the technique of making logical connections when there are no linking words.

Allow five minutes for this activity.

KEY

1 *like that* refers to taking out claws and filing down teeth.
2 The three expressions fit into the text as follows:
   I wouldn't dream of hurting a wild animal like that and I don't know any other vet who would do it either. You say you will give him to a zoo when he gets too big but a) *if he went to a zoo* with no claws he couldn't be put in with other lions – b) *because* he'd have no means of self-defence and c) *so* he'd be killed.

Exam practice: Part 2 Multiple choice comprehension questions

Allow ten minutes for this activity, which should be very straightforward.

> **KEY**
>
> 1 D 'It's my morning at the zoo,' said Maurice, who is clearly a vet on duty. He uses the occasion to take his friend to see the lion cub. The new surroundings (C) relate to the cub, not Maurice or the zoo.
>
> 2 B This answer should be clear from the text analysis activity. The cub could still go to a zoo with no claws (A) but would be kept alone. There are no references to Maurice's competence (C) or to the cub's size (D).
>
> 3 C The key factor is that most zoos *have enough cubs as it is*. It is nothing to do with general overcrowding in zoos (B) or the cub's nature (A) or value (D).
>
> 4 C Maurice says that most zoos *have enough cubs as it is* and that they are *almost two a penny*. The man is shocked because he paid a hundred pounds for his cub.

Extension

Allow five to ten minutes for this activity. Students need not spend too long on the discussion although some might like to argue for one particular pet or another. Arguments from the animals' point of view towards being kept in captivity will be a useful lead-in to the next unit.

Unit 8 **Zooooooh!**

Look at the aims of the unit with the students. The idea of thinking about the style of the text might be new. This is an important issue, especially where students expect a different style from a similar sort of text in their own language.

Getting an overall picture

1 Allow about five minutes for the discussion of the three questions. Make sure students do not refer to the text to answer the questions at this stage.

If students need help, you could suggest:

1 Zoos are useful for scientists to study animals and to keep rare animals from extinction.

2 Zoos keep animals in cramped, unnatural surroundings.

3 Encourage a moment or two of fun while students say *Zooooooh!* in different ways. They could say it enthusiastically, as a way of calling someone, or as an expression of disgust, which is, presumably, what the author intended. A further reason for writing *zoo* in this way may be to attract the reader's attention.

Allow a further five minutes for students to read the first and last paragraphs of the text and to discuss the questions. Elicit information from the last paragraph which suggests that the writer is clearly against zoos because the meeting between people and animals which they bring about is unhealthy and unrelaxed.

2 Preparing for the style of a text is an important technique. The rather 'chatty' style of popular magazine articles may be unfamiliar to students, or it may be that the idea of dealing with a serious issue in an informal way is unusual. By preparing for the style of a text, students will be in a better position to understand the text properly.

Because of the title, students should have little difficulty in seeing that the article appeared in a popular magazine. If your students have a European first language, you may like to discuss the fact that words of Romance (Latin) origins are not so readily associated with popular writing as those of Germanic origin.

KEY

The sentences most likely to be in a popular magazine:

1 B *Why* is more direct (and therefore more informal) than *What is the reason?*; *maintaining* is a formal word and *maintaining caged animals* is more abstract (and therefore more scientific) than *lying in a cage.*

2 A The contraction *There's* attempts to reproduce speech; *nothing like* is informal; the passive is more typical of formal writing.

3 B The passive is more formal; the epithet *good, bad, best in the world* between dashes and after *zoo*, as though added as an afterthought, suggests informal speech.

4 B The imperative is a feature of speech and less formal writing.

Analysing the text

Allow ten to fifteen minutes for the two activities.

1 Point out to students that, when a sentence begins with a participle, they need to find the subject of the sentence in order to understand it.

2

KEY

A <u>Having seen</u> wild animals close up, <u>zoo visitors</u> will be so enthusiastic about the wonders of the natural world that they will start to care deeply about what is happening to wild animals, go off and do something about it.

Rewritten:
Zoo visitors see wild animals close up and will be so enthusiastic about the wonders of the natural world that they will start to care deeply about what is happening to wild animals, go off and do something about it.

B <u>Robbed</u> of all its natural grace, <u>the animal</u> is shut into a space which is designed and controlled by people.

Rewritten:
The animal has been robbed of all its natural grace and is now shut into a space which is designed and controlled by people.

C <u>Saved</u> from having to earn its own living in the tough outside world, <u>it</u> has all its meals provided and doesn't even have to walk anywhere.

Rewritten:
It has been saved from having to earn its own living in the tough outside world and now has all its meals provided and doesn't even have to walk anywhere.

D <u>Having spent</u> hours watching people watching animals, <u>I</u> don't believe that any zoo can fulfil the high-minded educational aim it says it has.

Rewritten:
I have spent hours watching people watching animals and I don't believe that any zoo can fulfil the high-minded educational aim it says it has.

Exam practice: Part 3 Gapped text

Allow five to ten minutes for this activity.
The text analysis activity should help students to put the seven sentences into the correct space.

KEY
1 H The sentence introduces the theme of modern sensitivity to wildlife.
2 C The sentence illustrates the tiger's comfortable life.
3 F The sentence generalises from the particular instance given in the text.
4 A *close up* is synonymous with *face to face*.
5 D *no zoo* in the following sentence picks up *any zoo* in this one.
6 B The sentence explains the point about *true understanding*.
7 E The sentence repeats the 'imperative' formula.

Extension

Allow five to ten minutes for the discussion. This should provide a more relaxed activity, after the concentration of the preceding three. If students need help, you could suggest:
1 Possible alternatives to zoos are safari parks and nature reserves.
3 Some people think we should keep animals in cages for scientific experiments.
4 Zoos which are losing customers put it down to the simple fact that there are many other kinds of entertainment on offer.

Unit 9 A different point of view

Look at the aims of the unit with students. Ask them to recall techniques for getting an overall picture. Remind them of what is meant by *linking words*.

Getting an overall picture

The aim of these activities is to combine the technique of using the title with the techniques of using the first sentence of each paragraph and scanning for recurrent words.

1 Students could begin by talking about belongings they have with them in the classroom. If necessary, suggest that *your owner* might be the landlord of your house/flat or the boss of your company.

2 Allow ten minutes for students to read the first paragraph and to discuss the question. As usual, it is important at this stage that students realise it is not a case of finding the right answer in the text, only of discussing the questions so as to form a picture within which to read the text.

The following points should, however, emerge:
1 The *owner* in the title is any dog owner.
2 The text is supposed to be written for dogs.
3 The text may have been written for dog owners or perhaps for people who are thinking of getting a dog.
4 The purpose could be to inform and give advice.
5 Possible answers to this include treating your dog carefully, feeding it regularly, giving it plenty of exercise.

Responding to the text

Allow students ten minutes to read the text and do the activity.

Students should do the first part of this activity individually and then compare notes with other students when they have finished.

> **KEY**
>
> imagine – think
> cleverness – intelligence
> language – a set of sounds which carry meaning from the order in
>   which they are placed
> place – territory
> brought up – raised
> a language course at school – special training
> reading – concentrating on
> the noises dogs make – our communicatory sounds
> a sign which means 'hello' – a greeting gesture
> to manage to live with people – to fit in with a human pack
> to give up – deny
> real identity – true nature

Analysing the text

The aim of these activities is to remind students of how important it is
to interpret linking words and phrases correctly. It is particularly
important with linking words such as *if*, which is commonly taught only
as starting conditional phrases. In the example given here, its function is
slightly different.

Allow ten minutes for the activities.

1

> **KEY**
>
> 1 b)
> 2 c)
> 3 a)

2

> **KEY**
>
> 1 a) because of the meaning of *therefore*
> 2 a) because of the meaning of *in doing so*
> 3 b) because of the meaning of *if you are going to be at all happy*

Exam practice: Part 1 Multiple matching

Allow five to ten minutes for this activity. The synonym activity on page 44 should have helped students to reach the right conclusions quickly.

KEY

1 C *Cleverer* and *imagine* are synonymous with *a high level of intelligence* and *think*.
2 A Most of the paragraph is about speaking, different languages, language courses, writing and reading.
3 D The paragraph deals with the extent to which dogs understand language and to which humans understand dogs.
4 G *gesture* and *sign* are synonymous here.
5 F *identity crisis* is suggested by *deny your true nature*.
6 E The paragraph uses the word *choice* and contrasts the lack of choice which animals have with the choices humans can make.

Extension

Allow ten minutes for the discussion.

KEY

1 Dogs beg with a gesture similar to a pleading gesture in some cultures. They cock their heads to listen intently, like humans.
2 The writer seems to be saying to dog owners that they should respect their dog's intelligence and its need to be a dog.

Unit 10 How to get a laugh

Look at the aims of the unit with students. They should be clear.

Getting an overall picture

1 These activities should provide students with some meaningful listening practice as well as introduce the topic. Allow five to ten minutes for the activities.

Some students could try telling their own funny stories in English.

2 Make sure you give students only one minute to look over the text. As with all the activities aimed at getting an overall picture, it is very important that students do not start reading intensively at this stage.

You could help students by pointing out the first secret is *developing your own style* (lines 17–18).

If very few students have found any secrets after one minute, allow them to look at the text for a further one or two minutes. You could help them by telling them to look for *Perret* followed by *suggests* or *recommends* or *says*.

KEY

lines 17–18	*developing your own style*
line 18	*learning a few tricks*
lines 20–21	*build up a 'comedy collection'*
line 24	*Don't try to be what you're not.*
lines 30–31	*looking for material from your own experience*
line 38	*Material should also fit the audience.*
lines 43–44	*The more humour fits a particular situation, the funnier it is*
lines 53–54	*forget the idea that a speech should open and close with a joke*
line 55	*Sticking to rules like that could mean insecurity.*

Give students five to ten minutes to think of examples for the secrets. The aim of the activity is to think up a 'text' before reading the actual text.

Responding to the text

Allow fifteen minutes for students to read the text and discuss the summary sentences.

Try to organise the class so that students who read at roughly the same speeds are sitting together. It is very important that they think of their summaries before reading those offered.

If there are any difficulties with vocabulary, get students to apply one of the vocabulary guessing or avoiding techniques practised earlier in the course.

KEY

Paragraphs 1–2 a) *Some people can't tell a joke to save their lives* (lines 14–15) means that some people find telling jokes impossible; it has nothing to do with saving lives (b and c).

Paragraphs 3–4 c) The first step is to find funny material which is matched to yourself, not other people; then you should look out for humour within your family, not try out humour in your family (a). After the first 25 jokes, you should look out for humour everywhere, including your own experience, but not limiting yourself to your experience (b).

Paragraphs 5–6 a) The copying machine story was not liked by at least one member of the audience – the manager (b). The example of humour in paragraph 6 does not solely concern managers (c).

Paragraph 7 b) Perret advises people to forget the idea that a speech should open and close with a joke (a). Jokes can strengthen speeches, but the jokes themselves should not necessarily be strong (c).

Exam practice: Part 1 Multiple matching

The previous summarising activity (on page 47) should have helped students to match headings correctly. Allow five to ten minutes for the activity.

KEY

1 B *Suddenly Perret's ears stood up* shows that his attention was caught.
2 E *everyone* is repeated in the paragraph; learning *to use humour effectively* suggests that humour is a tool.
3 C *Do what suits you* means the same as *Don't try to be what you're not*.
4 A The paragraph is about using your own experience, your own life, as a source of material.
5 D *fit* means about the same as *match* in this context.
6 F The summary activity should have led students to the *attack* idea in this paragraph.
7 H *public speaking* refers to the speech making that the paragraph is about.

Extension

Allow five minutes for the discussion. If it is difficult for students to get going, you could ask them, for example, if they ever make jokes with each other before exams or tests. Some people don't like jokes about plane crashes, for example, if they are about to take a plane, while others find it helps relieve the tension.

Unit 11 **Superstar**

The aims of the unit should be quite clear.

Getting an overall picture

1 The aim of this activity is to encourage students to think about what they already know about the subject of a text before intensive reading.

Allow students five minutes to complete the paragraph. Make sure that they do not refer to the text: the idea, as always, is for them to think about information which they might find in the text before they read it intensively. As a result, almost anything reasonable can go in the gaps in the paragraph; students can then confirm or overturn their ideas when they start reading.

KEY

Possible answers:

Madonna was an international *star* in the 80s and early 90s. Although she was mostly famous for *singing*, she also *acted* and wrote *music*. It is less well-known that she was a *dancer* and can play three *instruments*.

---

2 Allow five to ten minutes for this activity. For students who are not familiar with 'word spiders', explain that Madonna is in the centre, as all the words are about her, and that the lines going from *Madonna* lead to main headings, which list her talents. These headings (all of which are provided) have lines leading to sub-headings (which students should complete with the words in the box).

Ask students to add any more words of their own to the spider. It is important that they think about all the categories so that they will be prepared to guess unknown words when it comes to reading.

KEY

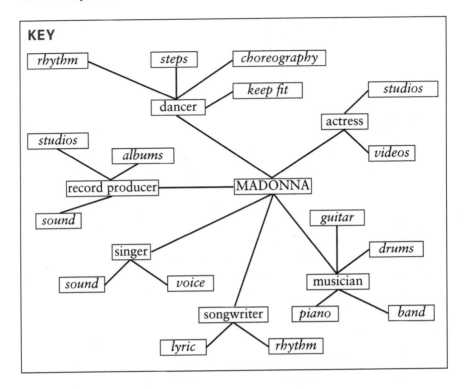

Responding to the text

Allow ten minutes for this activity. The choice of scenes is, of course, open to opinion. It is important to encourage discussion and for students to be able to justify their choice of pictures, according to their interpretation of the text.

KEY

Possible answers:

Paragraph 1 Madonna on stage in a stadium (scene 5)
Paragraph 3 young people in a disco (scene 2),
            Madonna in a recording studio (scene 6)
Paragraph 4 Madonna playing a guitar (scene 9)
Paragraph 5 Madonna sitting at the piano with another person,
            writing music (scene 1)
Paragraph 6 Madonna at the microphone in a small club (scene 4)

The unused scenes would be the New York–Manhattan skyline (scene 7) and the girls in a dancing class (scenes 3 and 8).

Analysing the text

The aim of the activities is to get students to see the discourse structure of the text; the structure is mainly a series of ends connected to means.

1 Students could work together to connect the achievements/ends to the means. Alternatively, they could do this individually and then discuss the results later.

KEY

Achievements (what she has done)	Means (how she has done it)
1 She has achieved success as a dancer.	She trained as a dancer.
2 She dances to a high standard.	She has a sense of rhythm.
3 She is a good video-maker.	She trained as a dancer.
4 She has written distinctive songs.	She knew her own voice and the importance of rhythm.
5 She has a professional approach to choreography.	She had years of dance training.
6 She can spend days working in the studios without a break.	The daily discipline of dance training.

2

KEY

Since (line 26) is followed by a means. The other expressions are followed by achievements.

Exam practice: Part 2 Multiple choice comprehension questions

The text analysis activities should have helped students to answer these questions. Allow five to ten minutes.

KEY

1 C She could dance before going to New York (A). The text says
she was *no 'disco-queen', picking up a few steps at the local
keep-fit class* (B). All her teachers were true professionals (D).
2 C Madonna's sense of rhythm made her a successful dancer, not
vice versa (A). The videos mentioned are not specifically dance
videos (B). Independence is not mentioned in the context of
touring (D).
3 A Collaboration with others is mentioned after the author has
given the reasons for Madonna's success as a songwriter (B).
Learning to play musical instruments seems to be a reason for
her success as a singer, not a songwriter (C). *distinctive* and
serious describe, in the text, Madonna's songs, not her
personality (D).
4 B Not all her songs are entirely her own work (A). Her songs
were based on dance styles at first but are not necessarily based
on them now (C). *she is responsible for such classics* does not
imply that she has not been responsible for other songs (D).

Extension

Allow five to ten minutes for the discussion. If students are particularly
interested in either Madonna, or stardom in general, they could present
their points of view in response to question 1 in a formal debate.

Unit 12 Success in a man's world

Discuss the aims of the unit with students. Reassure students, if necessary, that they will be given help in analysing the writer's intentions.

Getting an overall picture

1–2 The aim of these activities is to introduce the topic of the text and the vocabulary of football and of women in sport in general.

Allow about five minutes for these activities. Students will see that the photograph is unusual in that the footballer is a woman. The vocabulary work could be done in pairs. The vocabulary is for recognition only; translation dictionaries will be good enough for unknown words, or you could help students yourself. Try not to spend too long on the vocabulary items, so that the main point of the lesson is not missed. The words *racket* (connected with tennis) and *pedal* (part of a bicycle) are not about football.

3 As always in the pre-reading stage, it is important that students do not try to read every word of the text. Give them one minute only to find any words beginning with a capital letter.

If students have difficulty remembering names from the text, you could allow them to keep their books open; it is important, however, that they do not read about the names but simply write them down.

Students will probably remember the better-known names, like France, Italy and Scotland, but may need to look again to get the lesser-known ones.

> **KEY**
>
> *The list should look like this:*
> Trani (headline)   Rose Reilly (line 6)   Italian (line 9)
> France (line 13)   Italy (line 13)   Mary (line 31)
> Stewarton (line 33)   Scotland (line 34)
> Commonwealth Games (lines 40–41)   Edinburgh (line 41)
> *Daily Record* (line 45)   English (line 57)

Allow five to ten minutes for the sentence completion and discussion. As the instruction suggests, there are several possibilities for the sentences; it will be useful if students come up with different possibilities so that they can discuss which ones are true in their groups.

Do not tell students, at this stage, which of their sentences are true, so that reading the text will become, in part, a discovery.

Responding to the text

The aim of the reading phase of this activity is to remind students to read intensively by responding to the text.

Allow five to ten minutes for students to read the text and discuss the questions.

KEY

The journalist is presumably interested in entertaining a non-specialist audience. The overall feel is definitely that of a human interest story about someone a little unusual (b).

Analysing the text

The aim of these activities is to encourage students to look carefully at verb tenses and reference words when they are analysing text. This is particularly important for Part 3 of the exam. Make sure students are aware that whole paragraphs are missing from the text, not just sentences.

1 Allow students five minutes to look at the first three paragraphs and answer the questions.

KEY

The first three paragraphs make extensive use of present tenses – present simple and present perfect. The rest of the article uses mainly past tenses. This is very typical of this type of article. You would expect to find mainly present tenses in the first two missing paragraphs.

---

2 Remind students of previous units where they have used reference words to analyse texts. This activity practises the same skill. Allow students five minutes to find the reference words and answer the question.

KEY

Rose Reilly knows the answers to (these) questions

She can't explain why she (did)

You would expect to find a reference to questions in missing paragraph 2 and something about Rose's past in missing paragraph 3.

Exam practice: Part 3 Gapped text

Allow students ten minutes for this activity. They should already have a fair idea of where to put paragraphs A, D and G from the text analysis activity.

KEY

1 D Paragraph D uses present tenses and continues with the introduction theme.

2 A *a country* refers to Italy. *questions about football* are referred to in the following paragraph as *these questions*.

3 G Paragraph G finishes with *Rose chose*, referred to in the following paragraph by *She can't explain why she did.*

4 C In paragraph C Rose Reilly is quoted talking about her childhood at the age of 12. The preceding paragraph is about her early childhood and the following paragraph has Rose at the age of 16.

5 B Paragraph B refers back to the decision Rose had to make between football and athletics.

6 F Paragraph F refers back to France. *But then I made a big decision not to go back home* refers back, by contrast, to *I used to cry at night.*

Extension

Allow five minutes for the discussion. The discussion is intended to provide some relaxation after the intensity of the last two tasks. Alternatively, set question 2 as an essay question.

Unit 13 Film reviews

Discuss the aims with students. Remind them of 'text type' categories such as newspaper articles, brochures and here reviews in a magazine.

Keeping your purpose in mind

The aim of the activity is to help students to prepare for keeping their purpose in mind in Part 4 of the exam by thinking about the text type and the likely content of the text. You could remind students of the activity they did in Unit 8 on page 38 where they predicted the style of language on the basis of the text type.

Allow five to ten minutes for the activity.

KEY

Possible answers:

	Normally in a film review	Not normally in a film review
1 The reviewer's opinion of the film	✓	
2 The plot or story	✓	
3 A biography of the main actor		✓
4 A brief description of the main characters	✓	
5 Technical information about the cameras		✓
6 The audience's opinion of the film		✓
7 Comparisons with other films	✓	
8 The type of film it is	✓	

Exam practice: Part 4 Multiple matching – preparing by predicting

The aim of these activities is to help students prepare for Part 4 of the exam by thinking about the tasks beforehand and trying to predict what the text will be about before they start.

Allow ten to fifteen minutes for the activities.

1 Allow students five minutes to check the questions.

2

> **KEY**
>
> *Possible answers:*
>
> science fiction – usually about the future where a new discovery or invention has disastrous consequences for humans (*Jurassic Park, Men in Black*)
>
> romance – a love story (*The English Patient*)
>
> courtroom drama – the story includes many scenes inside a court of law; the hero is usually the accused and is often found to be innocent (*Kramer vs Kramer*)
>
> documentary – non-fiction film, though often dramatised (*Schindler's List*)
>
> biography – the story relates the life of someone (*Evita*)

3

> **KEY**
>
> A summary of the plot contains information about what takes place in the film; the reviewer's opinion offers the reviewer's personal view of the film.
>
> 1 the film fails   O
> 2 Sam saves the world   P
> 3 little more than competent   O
> 4 they all become victims   P
> 5 it charts his life and career   P
> 6 it is a bit over-sweet   O

Exam practice: Part 4 Multiple matching – reading to time

1 Be strict about the two minutes: the aim is for students to get realistic practice in organising their time. You could point out that they have used the underlining or highlighting technique before but you may need to emphasise to students the importance of moving on quickly when they do not understand something.

KEY

Possible highlighted sections of film A are:

little more than a competent TV movie   lawyer   case   trial   juries
the film fails to develop any strong commentary

The film is a courtroom drama (4) and the critic's opinion is that it is
well directed but weak (13).

When students have finished the task you could ask for a little
feedback on how easy or difficult it was.

2 Once again, be strict about allowing students only ten minutes to
complete the reading and the questions.

KEY

1 B *scientist (...) killer virus*
2 F *the murderer is in fact a monster related to a horrific creature
      of South American mythology*
3 D *he falls in love (...) a story of frustrated love*
4 A *lawyer (...) case (...) trial (...) juries*
5 E *This documentary*
6 C *the true story of Sister Helen Prejean*
7 E *charts Mandela's life and career*
8 C *the (...) story of (...), a nun who wrote of two condemned
       murderers whom she visited*
9 D *Every time something goes right (...), something goes wrong
       within five minutes.*
10 B *Can Sam save the world from the killer virus?*
11 F *After the terrible murder (...) the police (...) realise that the
       murderer is (...) a monster*
12 E *a bit over-sweet (...) too much of a nice old man*
13 A *little more than a competent TV movie (...) the film fails to
       develop any strong commentary*
14 F *what you have is just blood and violence, and that's what
       The Relic is*
15 C *A near faultless movie.*

Extension

As usual, the aim is simply to provide something more relaxing and to
round off the topic.

Unit 14 Goodbye to film heroes

Discuss the aims with students.

Getting an overall picture

1 The aim of this activity is to familiarise students with the idea of a *stunt* person. Allow five to ten minutes for reading and answering the questions.

> **KEY**
>
> 1 Stuntmen and stuntwomen fell from the sky, swam with sharks, rolled cars, fought, fell from high places and set fire to themselves.
> 2 Stuntmen and women are losing their jobs because their stunts are being replaced by computer-generated ones.

2 The aim of this activity is to practise using recurrent words to get an overall picture. It is important to point out that students should not look back to the text in order to answer the questions. The aim is, as always, to start thinking about the topic in order to make reading more effective later.

> **KEY**
>
> *Underlined or highlighted phrases*:
>
> Stuntmen and stuntwomen who entertained cinemagoers by falling from the sky, swimming with sharks and rolling fast cars have been replaced by technology (...) the people behind the top actors' most exciting scenes have had nearly all their work substituted by computer-generated stunts
>
> the most dangerous and costly stunts can be achieved by mixing computer graphics with live action
>
> The end of the stuntman was signalled by blockbusters such as *Volcano*
>
> Wayne Michaels, one of Britain's top stunt co-ordinators (...) at first studios tended to use computers for more extravagant stunts
>
> As a result, stunt people are becoming extinct.

In the mid-1990s there were 12,000 registered stunt people (...)
Loren Janes, a co-founder of the Stuntmen's Association of Motion
Pictures and Television (...) teams of stuntmen and stuntwomen had
found their work curtailed by technology

Computer technology pioneered in movies such as *Terminator 2* fell
in price and became capable of creating stunts which would either be
too expensive or too dangerous to attempt.

insurance companies became more reluctant to cover genuine stunts
(...) 'the companies will not insure real stunts,' said Simon Crane, a
veteran stunt co-ordinator

Many in the industry believe stunt people should develop expertise in
the new technology, acting as advisers on the virtual stunts. Some,
however, think that stuntmen can survive in their traditional careers.
Peter Brayham, a British stunt veteran who drove a car through a
plate-glass window (...) 'We call successful stunts "setting the
audience alight". The audience won't accept cartoon stunts for too
long.'

Possible answers:
1 He or she organises stunts and stunt people.
2 *Superman* films, *The Mask, Men in Black* are all full of them.
3 There will soon be no stunt people left.
4 Genuine stunts involve real people – they are not computer-
   generated.
5 It could be a stunt in a cartoon film – or a stunt that looks like
   something that would normally happen in a cartoon film.

Dealing with difficult words

The aim of this activity is to extend and consolidate students' word-
guessing skills. You could remind them of the techniques they have been
introduced to – taking words apart and looking at the immediate
context.

Allow five to ten minutes for the activity.

> **KEY**
>
> 1 *The Lost World* is mentioned along with other films, so *sequel* must be a film of some sort.
> 2 This word seems to be in opposition to *extravagant* and is linked to *common*. It is a near synonym of *common* in this context.
> 3 The following quotation says that stunt people would start work on a film but get sent home after only a few days. So *curtailed* means *cut short*.
> 4 This obviously describes *window*; if you could drive a car through it, the window must have been very big. So *plate-glass* means a large sheet of glass.

Responding to the text

The aim of this activity is to link interactive reading to completing the gapped text task in Part 3 of the exam. The activity is very similar to the one in Unit 4, where students had to role-play interviewing the writer.

The answers to the questions are not in the text: students must invent answers by interacting with the text.

Allow students ten minutes or more for the activity.

> **KEY**
>
> *Possible answers:*
>
> 1 You can see real actors doing what looks like very dangerous stunts.
> 2 Probably they were the first films to use computer graphics mixed with live action.
> 3 Bitter? Sad? Resigned?
> 4 Because they had discovered they could achieve the same effects more cheaply on computer.
> 5 This question is completely open.
> 6 Find another job? Work without insurance?
> 7 No.

Exam practice: Part 3 Gapped text

After thinking through the questions in the previous section, students should be able to do the gapfill quickly. Allow no more than five minutes.

KEY

1 C
2 A
3 G
4 D
5 B
6 H
7 F

C, A, D and F are paraphrases of the answers to questions 1, 2, 4 and 7 in the previous task.
G fits the context appropriately.
B is an example of a dangerous stunt.
H is the answer to question 6 in the previous task.

Extension

Allow students ten minutes for the discussion. If students need some prompting for questions 3 and 4 you could suggest *firefighters* and *soldiers* for 3, *typographers, cartoonists, bank clerks, telephonists,* etc., for 4.

Unit 15 How to be a movie star

Discuss the aims with students. The 'comparing opinions' activity is similar to the 'relating to personal experience' activity in Unit 3.

Getting an overall picture

1 Allow students a few minutes to look at the text introduction.

2 Allow students five to ten minutes to discuss the questions. Obviously there are no 'right' answers. You could ask students to make a note of their answers as they will need to refer back to them when they read the text.

Responding to the text

The aim of these activities, as with other interactive reading in this book, is to help students to get a good idea of what the text is about by responding to it appropriately. This will help when choosing the correct summary for each paragraph.

1 Allow five to ten minutes for this activity.

KEY

Possible underlined or highlighted phrases:

Opinion 1 what usually happens is that they present word-heavy performances that represent nothing they have either seen on screen or experienced in real life

Opinion 2 if the actor wants to convey extra information with a facial expression, the best time to do this is before the speech

Opinion 3 You will be very impressed with what wonderful, truthful and subtle performances you have put on the screen even though you know the person swallowing was not feeling a thing

One actor was upset, claiming that she hated watching actors pull faces and that listening should be what we would do in real life. I immediately got her with another actor and told her not to listen to what he was saying, but to spend her energies in giving a whole range of expressions. When I asked her 'How was that?' she replied 'Terrible', but we all – the other actors and I in chorus – went 'It was wonderful!'. Which it was.

In order to achieve good results with gestures, you have to get good
at them – and that means research and practice. Research means
watching yourself in real-life situations and finding out what is your
vocabulary of moves and gestures. Watch other people in the
underground, in shops, at parties (...) Then watch screens, see what
other actors do

2 Allow five to ten minutes for this activity.

Analysing the text

Students often have difficulties with noun phrases starting with *what*.
The aim of these activities is to help students to understand these
phrases. Allow ten minutes for the activities.

1

> **KEY**
>
> 1 the thing that
> 2 the things
> 3 the
> 4 (nothing)

2

> **KEY**
>
> 1 the expression
> 2 the thing that, the other person's thoughts and emotions
> 3 a very commonly observed scene
> 4 our normal activity

Exam practice: Part 1 Multiple matching

Students should be able to do this very quickly, having by now got a
good idea of the text. Allow five minutes.

```
KEY
1  H
2  C
3  B
4  E
5  F
6  G
7  D
```

Extension

Allow students five to ten minutes for the discussion.

Review unit

The aim of this Review unit is to remind students of all the reading techniques presented and practised in the rest of the book.

Getting an overall picture

Allow ten minutes for this activity. Ask students to try to remember the techniques for getting an overall picture before they look at the anagrams. (There is a technique for getting an overall picture in most units.)

KEY

1 frequent   2 pictures, diagrams   3 title   4 introduction
5 paragraph, lines   6 capital   7 knowledge   8 style

Possible answers:

Text type	Technique
stories	1, 5
biographies	1, 5, 7
newspaper and magazine articles	2, 3, 5, 6, 8
non-fiction books	2, 3, 4, 5

Other techniques covered in the book are reading the first and last paragraphs (Unit 8) and using subtitles (Unit 10).

When you have got an overall picture, you should spend some time thinking about the possible content of the text before starting to read intensively.

Responding to the text

1 Allow ten to fifteen minutes for this activity. When students have finished the team game they could quickly discuss together which of the techniques they have found most useful in their general reading.

> **KEY**
>
> **relate** (Exam Tip 8) relate ideas in non-fiction texts to your own experience
> **form** (Exam Tip 18) form an opinion of the characters in stories
> **rephrase** (Exam Tip 23) rephrase sections of the text in ways which are easier for you to understand
> **summarise** (Exam Tip 26) summarise each paragraph of a text as you read
> **visualise** (Exam Tip 28) try to visualise what the text describes
> **ask** (Exam Tip 38) ask intelligent questions about the text as you read

Analysing the text

1 Allow ten minutes for this activity. Students could do the activity individually or in pairs.

> **KEY**
>
> 1 <u>Having found</u> the first exercise too difficult, ⓘ left it and went straight on to the second one.
> *Rewritten:* I found the first exercise too difficult and so I went straight on to the second one.
> 2 They both refer to exercises.
> 3 *Because* would fit before *If* (or *Since* or *As*). There is clearly an implied effect–cause relationship between the two sentences.
> 4 It refers to an intention. The verb *was* refers to the past, not to a hypothetical situation.
> 5 The thing that

2 This activity reviews skill areas not covered in 1. Allow five minutes for the activity. Students can check their own answers.

> **KEY**
>
> 1 making logical connections from one part of the text to another
> 2 looking carefully at reference words

Keeping your purpose in mind and ignoring irrelevant information

This activity is as much of a test as it is a review activity. You could organise it as a competition to see which student can get the pieces of advice first. The activity should not take more than five minutes.

KEY

1 Use the information you are given about the text type to think about likely content.
2 Study the information you have to find in the text before you start reading.
3 Identify key words in the pre-reading briefing.
4 Underline words and expressions in the text which have a similar meaning to the key words.
5 Make an effort to predict words or phrases which are likely to be in the text.
6 Use your time wisely.

Dealing with difficult words

1 Allow ten minutes for this activity. Students could do the questionnaire in small groups, rather than pairs. The activity should not be taken too seriously!

2 a) answers generally take up the exam tips presented throughout the book. You could ask students to read back through Exam Tips 2, 11, 14, 15 and 37 to round off.

Practice tests

The information in this introduction to the five practice tests will help you plan how best to use them with your students.

A key point about them is that they can be used flexibly, in conjunction with or independently of the learning units. Test parts can be used in any order, individually or as a complete test:

- to check progress or to provide authentic timed exam practice.
- after every four learning units or at other intervals throughout the course.
- for homework or in class.
- with students working individually or in pairs/groups.

How to use the practice tests

Use this section in conjunction with the information on pages 8–9 of the Foundation unit to (re)familiarise students with Paper 1 of the FCE exam and introduce the five practice tests.

All the practice test material reflects one of the five unit themes and the 'Key to Themes' box will enable you to make the most of links with individual units. Note too that the practice tests cover all variants of Paper 1 in the FCE. Multiple matching of summary sentences (rather than headings) in Part 1 of the exam (covered in Unit 15) features in both Practice Test 2 and Practice Test 3, which also features gapped paragraphs (rather than sentences) in Part 3 (covered in Unit 12).

Try to give students plenty of practice in reading to time and make sure they are aware of the importance of this aspect. At least one practice test should be completed under full exam conditions before students sit the exam itself.

Remember your reading skills!

Encourage students to get into the habit of reminding themselves of the reading skills and strategies they can draw on to help them before they embark on any of the practice test material. This is a good way to prepare for the exam too, where the confidence students will gain from knowing what they know will stand them in good stead.

Practice test 1

Part 1

0 H

1 B The *seasonal and low paid* patterns of work in tourism *are changing fast.*

2 E The main point of the paragraph is that, despite the hard work, working in tourism gives you *the pleasure of knowing you have helped people.*

3 F The paragraph deals with *career options* in tourism which are *many and varied* so there are plenty to choose from.

4 C The paragraph is about courses which *equip you with the skills needed for a successful career in tourism.*

5 G The *new approach* is the new Higher National Diploma in Sustainable Tourism on offer from Newton Rigg College.

6 A The last paragraph is an invitation to *consider the possibilities of a career in tourism* and find yourself *pleasantly surprised.*

Part 2

7 D It was clearly not acting just out of obedience because it loved the command (A). *Like any obedient tracker-dog* suggests that the narrator was trained for the task (B). *The pavement was rich with smells* but there is no indication that the dog was frustrated by them (C).

8 B It was the fragrances that were complex, not the area (A). *stones* refers to the pavement, not the buildings (C). The pavements were *rich with smells,* but there is otherwise no indication of their condition (D).

9 C The object of this sentence is *one scent – among the many that lay about* refers back to and elaborates on this object so *many* cannot refer to new commands (A), difficult tasks (B) or onlookers (D).

10 A We know only that his shirt was smooth (B). The whisper was the noise of the caretaker's hand on his shirt, not the sound of his voice (C). He ran his hand over his stomach to show his authority, not because he was feeling unwell (D).

11 C The caretaker was *being clever* in his display of authority; there is no connection between this and the lack of weapon (A). The caretaker was not wearing a badge – *he handled his stomach as though it was a badge* (B). The fact that the caretaker was *ageing* is mentioned in passing, not in connection with the whisper-like noise (D).

12 B He tells the owner he is wasting his time, so is not encouraging (A). The police *would never have thought of using a tracker-dog* because it was *impossible* (C). The *crossword puzzle* is an impossible task, not a game (D).

13 B The sense of smell is compared on equal terms with the sense of hearing (A). *If Sherlock Holmes ...* does not set a condition. A dog does not need even to see the person in order to get all the details (C). The dog says it is difficult to distinguish scents but it does not say that it is impossible (D).

14 A A dog can tell you many things about someone it has not seen but not without seeing you (B). *provided* (line 36) means *as long as* – it is not the past of *provide* (C). The passage speaks only about a dog's investigative power (D).

Part 3

0 I

15 F *the holiday* refers back to the first paragraph and the *fishery* is *the place* in the next sentence.

16 C The time scale gives the clue to this one: he saw the house, decided to buy it and then quit his job and bought it.

17 D He couldn't move his arms and legs as a result of the collapse.

18 B Grammatically, sentence B copies the previous sentence: *I had no ...* Having *no experience of running any kind of enterprise and no background in agriculture or fisheries* constituted the *huge risk.*

19 A Sentence A explains why *we didn't suffer much*, describing life in London to compare with life in Ireland in the next sentence.

20 E *We're never going to get rich* in the next sentence illustrates *he's yet to make a profit* in sentence E.

21 H *that* in *People tend to forget that* refers to *You're just swapping the old life for a different set of pressures* in sentence H.

Part 4

0 F

22 C Thame Park was the home of a fiancé of one of King George III's sons.

23 B *One screening was interrupted by a shout of recognition.*

24 D *a combination of gardens from the north and south of England, and at Pinewood Studios*

25 F The film was *Rob Roy – which arrived just a few weeks later.*

26 E The director *was astonished to find how well preserved it was – 'They haven't done any alterations'.*

27 F *There was a lot of discussion ...*

28 E The director *changed his shooting script to maximise the use of the location.*

29 A The palace appeared *as an opera house.*

30 D *The building has now been converted into flats.*

31 C The *Japanese consortium which had bought it went bankrupt* and *it was just left to fall down.*

32 C Thame Park is a *mixture of houses – eighteenth century and Tudor and medieval.*

33 A *We didn't have to worry about traffic.*

34 B *Bookings have increased tremendously* at the Crown Hotel.

35 D One of the gardens *was laid out in the studios* for use *if rain prevented filming.*

Practice test 2

Part 1

0 I

1 C *Getting permission* is synonymous with *I check if it's okay.*

2 A The first and the third sentences of the paragraph clearly describe the two methods.

3 F The dog (an animal) spoke to the writer about spending the day on the sofa. Its owner repeated, or confirmed this. The same thing happened about *talking when she does the washing-up.*

4 B Laszlo is the other animal professional. *Now we listen,* he says.

5 E The *solutions* consisted of pills for the dog and its owners, and giving the dog a different name.

6 H The contradiction is that the writer eats meat and feels *guilty about not being a vegetarian.* She goes on to explain her behaviour in two different ways.

7 D She says that she closes herself down – in other words, she doesn't use her powers all the time, for fear of being *dead in a day.*

Part 2

8 A The report said he had *done his utmost* in preparing Margaret for a career (B). The school recommended her for university (C). If he encouraged her to go to Oxford University he obviously did not bring her up to work as a shopkeeper (D).

9 B She was brought up fifty yards away from where Margaret lived (A). She *lives where she was born,* not where Margaret was born (C). She has never moved (D).

10 C The reason and result clause *Not so serious that* shows that she did play with other children (A). *this is not a rags-to-riches story* (B). There is no mention of memory (D).

11 D Bernard Newman *came to talk about spies* but we do not find out if he was one (A). He gave a lecture but did not, as far as we know, help the girls with reading (B). He *asked for questions* but did not ask any questions himself – he did not test the girls at all (C).

12 B She spoke instead of the expected sixth-former, but there is no mention of her stopping anyone else (A). Her lack of appreciation of the humour has to be read in – there is no evidence for it here (C). She may have been impolite to her peers, but not to the lecturer (D).

13 A The written records do not refer to Margaret, but whether people referred to her at school or not is another question, not addressed here (B). The idea that written evidence has been hidden or that Margaret's name has been taken away have to be read in (C and D).

14 B She played with other children, she had parties, she was not deprived (A). She had potential, but there was *little early evidence* of it (C). The word *amusing* is used to describe Bernard Newman, not Margaret (D).

Part 3

  0 I

15 F Sentence F repeats *something* from the previous sentence, and *them* in the next sentence refers back to *eyes* in sentence F.

16 A Sentence A, and in particular *bodybuilder,* takes up the theme of *straining with muscle* and *Yet when I saw her, she didn't appear to have any muscles at all.*

17 E *That* in the next sentence refers to the fact that Demi Moore is *not actually better looking in the flesh than on screen.*

18 H The quotation in the next sentence picks up the words of sentence H.

19 B *the film* in sentence B refers back to *GI Jane.*

20 G *also* suggests that the article has already dealt with one aspect of Demi Moore's part in *GI Jane* – the fact that she refused to use a double.

21 D *she was never sure* in the previous sentence is picked up in the quotation in sentence D. In the next sentence, *so* refers to not having anything that was good enough.

Part 4

  0 D

22 B Placements abroad include *Mexico, the USA* and *Australia.*

23 B *combined with the application to business of computing*

24 E *how to apply information technology in a business context*

25 A One of the options is *intermediate French*. Going abroad is not mentioned.

26 D *If you have difficulties initially,* there are *remedial tutorials* and *you also have a personal tutor to help you.*

27 E *You will learn how to work with others* on a *practical course* which uses *real-life scenarios* in *case studies* and *group work.*

28 B Both disciplines are named.

29 B *most traineeships are in the UK*

30 E The course covers *tools to develop software applications and to bring new ideas quickly to life.*

31 C *You will also study the history and culture of Eastern and Central Europe.*

32 C *German* is available *for complete beginners and at a more advanced level.*

33 A *This course is particularly suitable for people with substantial work experience.*

34 D This is a *Foundation Course* which can lead on to a degree programme.

35 E This is *a practical course* with *three main areas of study* but no formal qualification at the end.

Practice test 3

Part 1

0 I

1 G The paragraph deals with how thoroughly Ivan Lendl has prepared for success, in every detail, throughout his life.

2 C The information about Jackie Stewart points to his reliability and attention to detail.

3 A The paragraph suggests that we should prepare even though we might get teased for it.

4 D Some people don't prepare so they have an excuse for not succeeding.

5 B Some people draw attention to their preparations so others will feel sorry for them if they fail.

6 H This paragraph gives examples of hard work leading to success.

7 F Christine Brinkley sacrificed her sleep to achieve success.

Part 2

8 C *Even if they lived within easy distance of one* suggests that some of them did, in fact, live close to a theatre (A). They did not use books because *they did not have enough English* (B). *they couldn't understand the captions* (D).

9 A *not to the same extent* means that not so many films were made, not that they were shorter (B). The growing demand for films was not generated by the war (C). Film production was given a low priority in Europe. We are not given any information about the priority of film production in America (D).

10 B There were no American art films – *Hollywood is not interested in art* (A). There is nothing in the text about how many American films were seen in the world, compared with other countries' films (C). America has never been *in the lead when it comes to developing film as an art form* (D).

11 D *There is nothing about this attitude that should make us look down on it* means that he does not despise it (A). The word *decent* is supposed to be applied to Hollywood films, just as it is applied to furniture. *You might wish he were* does not suggest that this is the writer's wish (B). The comparison with furniture is drawn to make the point that a serviceable film is as good as a serviceable piece of furniture (C).

12 C The subject of the sentence is *Hollywood*. The sentence starts *So Hollywood quickly recognised film*, so the object of the sentence is *film* and not *entertainment medium* (A), *Hollywood* (B) or *money* (D).

13 B Both *serious* and *not so serious* films attempt to fulfil the aims of expressionism (A). Expressionism was a German phenomenon in the 1920s (C). Expressionism aimed to show particular emotions, but not strange ones (D).

14 B *in the business of learning* simply means *interested in learning*: it does not suggest that Hollywood is more businesslike (A). Taking on and adapting ideas is not the same as copying them (C). Hollywood is far more interested in learning than in teaching (D).

Part 3

0 H

15 D *In reality* in sentence D refers back to *it must have seemed as if*.

16 F *that particular side to their character* in sentence F refers back to extraordinary strong-mindedness.

17 B *those adaptations* in sentence B refers back to *the efforts made by daughters to liven it up a bit, or even to make it a bit more modern.*

18 A *at least some minor misbehaviour* in sentence A refers back to *something wrong*.

19 G *Guilt* in sentence G obviously refers back to the previous paragraph.

20 C *The new breed of convent girls* in sentence C refers back to *today's convent girls* and *Nowadays*.

Part 4

0 F

21 C *Visit (…), a unique project using natural heat to generate electricity.*

22 A *Enjoy panoramic views (…) from the top of Mount Eden*

23 D *Visit (…), a replica of an old mining town*

24 A *enjoy a guided tour of the glow-worm grotto. Back up above ground*

25 F *You may wish to take a scenic flight*

26 D *Travel along the shores of Lake Hawea for lunch at the beautiful holiday resort of Queenstown. For the rest of the day*

27 D *relax and go shopping*

28 G *do some last-minute shopping*

29 B *See rainbow trout (...) view the rare flightless kiwi bird.*

30 C *on to the orchard and vineyard region*

31 G *view the Church of the Good Shepherd*

32 A *Dinner is a special Maori feast, typical of the region*

33 D *an endless choice of (...) traditional New Zealand restaurants*

34 C *board your inter-island cruise*

35 E *a launch cruise*

Practice test 4

Part 1

0 I

1 B The paragraph states that, according to a survey, every screen needs another source of income, popcorn, just to keep operating. Popcorn is the *life saver* that keeps cinemas open.

2 F The paragraph lists the costs of running a cinema. It is the *manager's challenge* to make the sums add up.

3 D The paragraph compares the *cost to the consumer* of popcorn in and out of the cinema.

4 C *Pleasure value* is how the price of popcorn in the cinema is explained.

5 A Managers are *learning to cash in*, that is *to sell more*, by *using the tricks of the supermarket and fast-food industry*.

6 E The paragraph traces popcorn back to its American origins.

7 H Sales of popcorn and soft drinks guarantee a profit, *no matter which film is showing*.

Part 2

8 A Although the text says that disobedience was encouraged, it is clear that there is a collusion between teacher and pupils (B). The school was *an odd place* because the pupils *learned odd things* – the building is not mentioned (C). The rules were different but they were not written by the pupils (D).

9 D The lesson was not about disobedience – *it was a forbidden lesson* (A). The lesson was *more delicious* than other children have had – but not necessarily the best in that school (B). The lesson was *delicious* because it was forbidden – not because it was about food. It was actually about a Polish king (C).

10 C The bell, called a *warning bell* later on, is clearly rung by the headteacher to show that an inspector is on his way. The pupils were enjoying the lesson, not wanting it to end (A). The teacher is obviously in league with the pupils, against the inspector (B). It is obvious that they are not interested in showing the inspector anything, only in hiding things from him (D).

11 B Manya's *voice was full of regret* as she talked about the king –
she *understood quite a lot* and so was not frustrated (A). She
feels regret before the lesson is interrupted – so she could not be
sad and angry (C). *her* in *tried to make her strong* refers to
Poland (D).

12 D Some children took books to the bedrooms, but presumably
came back (A). The way in which the activity is described
suggests organisation (B). The temperature is not referred to –
presumably the children *shivered* with emotion (C).

13 C The headteacher was *unhappy* and *in a panic* because she was
worried the children had not had *time to hide their disobedience*
– *making exquisite buttonholes* was a cover for this (A). The
children had not hidden their needlework – *there was no sign of
anything but needlework* (B). She was afraid the inspector had
walked so fast that the children would not have had *time to hide
their disobedience* (D).

14 A The inspector approved of the fairy tales being read – he did not
necessarily like them himself (B). Needlework was all there was
to be seen (C). The inspector had not given any warning – it was
the headteacher who had rung the bell (D).

Part 3

0 I

15 C Sentence C gives an example of how the *beauty and unspoilt
nature of the islands are carefully protected* and this is amplified
in the next sentence.

16 G *mass tourism, current policy* and *'quality visitor'* in sentence G
link directly with the next sentence.

17 B Sentence B is about *mass tourists* in contrast with the *perfect
tourist* in the previous sentence. The next sentence then gives an
example of the *disastrous consequences* of mass tourism.

18 D Sentence D identifies the source – *Atterville Ceydras* – and
theme – *nature* – of the quote in the next sentence.

19 A *all* in sentence A refers back to *they* (the tourists) in the previous
sentence and *do so* refers back to *put up with it* (nature) – the
text continues with an explanation and examples.

20 E *exotic* in sentence E refers to *the wonders of the world* in the
previous sentence and *exciting* refers to *adventures and safari*.

21 H *need not* and *would* in sentence H refer back to *spoils such
places* in the previous sentence.

Part 4

 0 B

22 E *Care of these cats is quite straightforward*

23 E *The fur of these cats is tipped, creating a reddish shade, which contrasts with the white underfur.*

24 A *You will need to (...) wipe their faces regularly (...) daily cleaning is equally essential.*

25 B *The Turkish Van is a breed with (...) distinctive markings (...) on the head, ears and tail.*

26 B *In the spring, the cats shed much of their long fur*

27 C *In the winter, when their fur is at its longest*

28 C *These are (...) active cats*

29 D *they must have plenty of exercise*

30 A *These are all large cats*

31 E *These breeds are both considerably larger than the average cross-bred cat.*

32 D *Oriental Shorthair cats (...) positively demand affection*

33 D *they may (...) amuse themselves, by shredding the curtains*

34 C *These are intelligent (...) cats*

35 A *the odd-eyed white, which has one blue eye and one orange eye*

Practice test 5

Part 1

0 I

1 F The family's *first lesson* is that the ready-made course which they bought for their daughter Kate *was not what she needed.*

2 D The paragraph discusses how the family looked at where they would be in order to decide on the education programme for their children.

3 A The paragraph describes how they tackle the study of mathematics.

4 E The *diary, journal* and *newsletter* are *a personal record.*

5 G The paragraph is about the space on the boat.

6 B *Hands-on learning experiences* suggests *learning by doing* – and all the examples illustrate this.

7 H *Team entertainment* summarises the drama production which children from different boats teamed up to put on.

Part 2

8 B The other people got ready for landing (A) and had conversations (C). The houses on the ground looked like toys from above – Juana did not have any toys (D).

9 C Her knowledge and studies did not make England *any more touchable* (A). Her mother's requests are mentioned in passing – she was not worried about them (B). Her *sick feeling* was not related to *the plane's dropping* (D).

10 A From the previous section you gather this was her first time in England (B). She had been away from home twice with friends – not to friends' houses (C). She went to Madrid, not Mallorca, when she was fourteen (D).

11 B She had never met Sandie (A and D). *They* in *They talked the same language* refers to Juana and her two friends, not just Katerine and Dolores (C).

12 D She had boasted about going, so did not say she would miss them (A). They would be doing the boring things, not her (B). She would remember them while she was shopping but would not necessarily buy them anything (C).

13 C The *boring summer* is associated with Juana's friends, not with *here and happening* (A). Juana is obviously thinking about the whole experience, not just the arrival at the airport (B). The shopping in King's Road is not yet happening, of course (D).

14 B The whole feeling of the text is one of uncertainty and apprehension. Juana does not seem curious – she does not, in the text, think about wanting to learn more (A). She does not express any regrets about having decided to go (C). Her sick feeling is brought on by the apprehension, not because she is ill (D).

Part 3

0 H

15 C *other domesticated creatures* in the next sentence suggests that *This* refers to a domestic animal.

16 F The next sentence expands on the theme of increasing *their share of the total living matter.*

17 A In the next sentence *those who argue that animals should have the same rights as humans* refers to *the animal rights movement.*

18 E *it* in *there is evidence to support it* refers to the *idea that domestication (…) has actually helped animals to survive.*

19 G Sentence G reiterates the theme of the previous sentence: *it was (…) the animals themselves who approached humans* is nearly synonymous with *it was animals that took the first step.*

20 D Sentence D expands on *the benefits* in the previous sentence and links in content and structure to the next sentence.

Part 4

0 D

21 B *care and maintenance of buildings and repairs*

22 E *delivering (…) on time is worth almost any amount of unpunctual genius*

23 A *If you can establish your expertise in a subject (…) that is in demand, your advice is taken more seriously than that of a (…) consultant who has never had to put into practice what he advises about.*

24 C *nothing impresses clients as much as a successful record*

25 C *An agent can be useful, here. It means that the commercial side of things is divorced from the personal*

26 A *It might be better to describe yourself as*

27 C *That is (...) a matter of personal contacts*

28 E *opportunities (...) seem to appear through personal contacts*

29 C *You should begin by looking round for clients who you think would like your work (...) studying media that publish the kind of thing you (...) can do.*

30 D *Sound investment advice is (...) important*

31 B *The opportunities to operate without declaring your income to the authorities are very considerable*

32 A *The term 'consultant' (...), in some potential clients' minds, means 'managers who are out of work and looking for a job'.*

33 D *Top names can make a great deal of money (...) The majority (...) earn much smaller amounts of money.*

34 B *put that message over in your publicity and (...) make sure it is seen by possible customers*

35 E *Journalism is a good area (...) particularly if you specialise in a technical subject (...) On the other hand, it is very difficult to break into more general fields*